Stories to See and Share

Stories to See and Share

Book 3

Maline C. Crockett
Illustrations by Nina Grover

Deseret Book Company
Salt Lake City, Utah

To all of my wonderful grandchildren

© 1993 Maline C. Crockett

All rights reserved. Permission is hereby granted WITH PURCHASE to reproduce any
part of this book on a limited basis for personal or church use only. Reproduction of any part
of this book for commercial use is forbidden unless permission is obtained in writing from the publisher,
Deseret Book Company, P. O. Box 30178, Salt Lake City, Utah 84130

Deseret Book is a registered trademark of Deseret Book Company.

ISBN 0-87579-677-X

Printed in the United States of America
10 9 8 7 6 5 4 3 2 1

Contents

Presentation 1
Temples—Appreciating the Purpose of Heavenly Father's Work

This presentation helps children appreciate and understand the reason we have temples throughout the world.

Presentation 2
Faith—Keeping the Commandments of Heavenly Father

This presentation helps children understand the basic definition of faith.

Presentation 3
Reverence—Showing Love for Heavenly Father

This presentation teaches children the difference between appropriate and inappropriate behavior in church.

Presentation 4
Prayer—Drawing Closer to Heavenly Father

This presentation teaches children the many different kinds of prayers and the importance of talking to their Heavenly Father.

Introduction

Four presentations which will help the leader or parent more effectively teach children the basic principles of the gospel are included in *Stories to See and Share, Book 3*. This is the third in a series of books now published for this purpose. Again, simple illustrations and basic concepts are the underlying motivations that will help children to learn. Simply told, these presentations provide a basic foundation from which children will expand the concepts of gospel teachings into a continual gospel study as they grow older.

Each presentation is designed to be given by the leader or parent or by one or more of the children themselves (older children enjoy holding up the pictures and telling the stories). Each presentation has a set of illustrations that are numbered and a set of captions with corresponding numbers.

For presentation 1, the captions can be glued to the backs of the pictures and then read while the pictures are held up before the children in the audience. For even more effective responses, the leader, parent, or children may memorize the captions.

Presentations 2, 3, and 4 offer alternate methods that can be used to add variety to the presentations.

It is my purpose to provide simple, illustrative concepts to help the leader or parent who wishes to teach more effectively through the use of visual presentations. To this end, may joy and happiness be yours as you accomplish this task.

Presentation 1

Temples—Appreciating the Purpose of Heavenly Father's Work

This presentation introduces children to our temples. It is planned so children will gain an appreciation for the purpose of temples as well as the tremendous effort it took to build them. The children are introduced to the basic concepts of temple ordinances and the reasons we participate in temple work.

Materials Needed:
2 poster boards, 24" x 30", any color
photocopies of illustrations and captions to be used (optional)
spray glue, glue stick, or rubber cement
felt-tip markers, colored pencils, or oil pastels
scissors

Directions:
1. Cut each poster board into fourths, making eight separate sheets.
2. Work from photocopies of the original illustrations and captions to keep the book intact for future presentations.
3. Color each picture with felt-tip markers, colored pencils, or oil pastels. (Tip: oil pastels are especially good for skin tones. Use tissue to smooth and blend them.)
4. Glue each picture to a piece of poster board, centering each one and pressing firmly to seal the materials together.
5. Cut each caption along the dotted lines.
6. Glue the appropriate caption in the upper left-hand corner on the back of each mounted picture for easy reading.

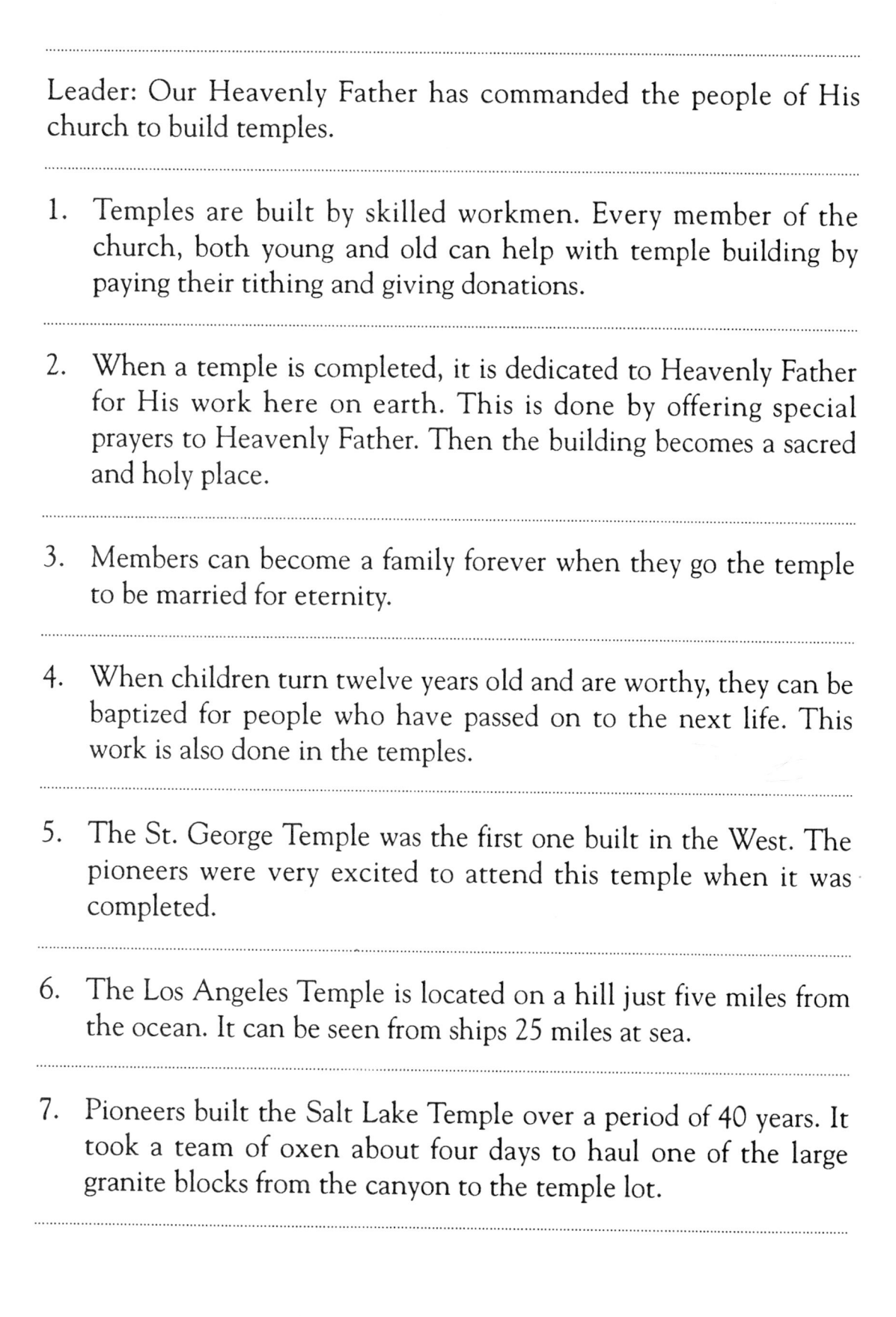

Leader: Our Heavenly Father has commanded the people of His church to build temples.

1. Temples are built by skilled workmen. Every member of the church, both young and old can help with temple building by paying their tithing and giving donations.

2. When a temple is completed, it is dedicated to Heavenly Father for His work here on earth. This is done by offering special prayers to Heavenly Father. Then the building becomes a sacred and holy place.

3. Members can become a family forever when they go the temple to be married for eternity.

4. When children turn twelve years old and are worthy, they can be baptized for people who have passed on to the next life. This work is also done in the temples.

5. The St. George Temple was the first one built in the West. The pioneers were very excited to attend this temple when it was completed.

6. The Los Angeles Temple is located on a hill just five miles from the ocean. It can be seen from ships 25 miles at sea.

7. Pioneers built the Salt Lake Temple over a period of 40 years. It took a team of oxen about four days to haul one of the large granite blocks from the canyon to the temple lot.

8. Heavenly Father wants all of His children to be able to go to His temples. Our church has built temples all over the world so all the worthy members can worship Him in the temples.

Leader: Those members of The Church of Jesus Christ of Latter-day Saints who keep Heavenly Father's commandments can enjoy special blessings by attending His temples.

No. 1

No. 2

No. 3

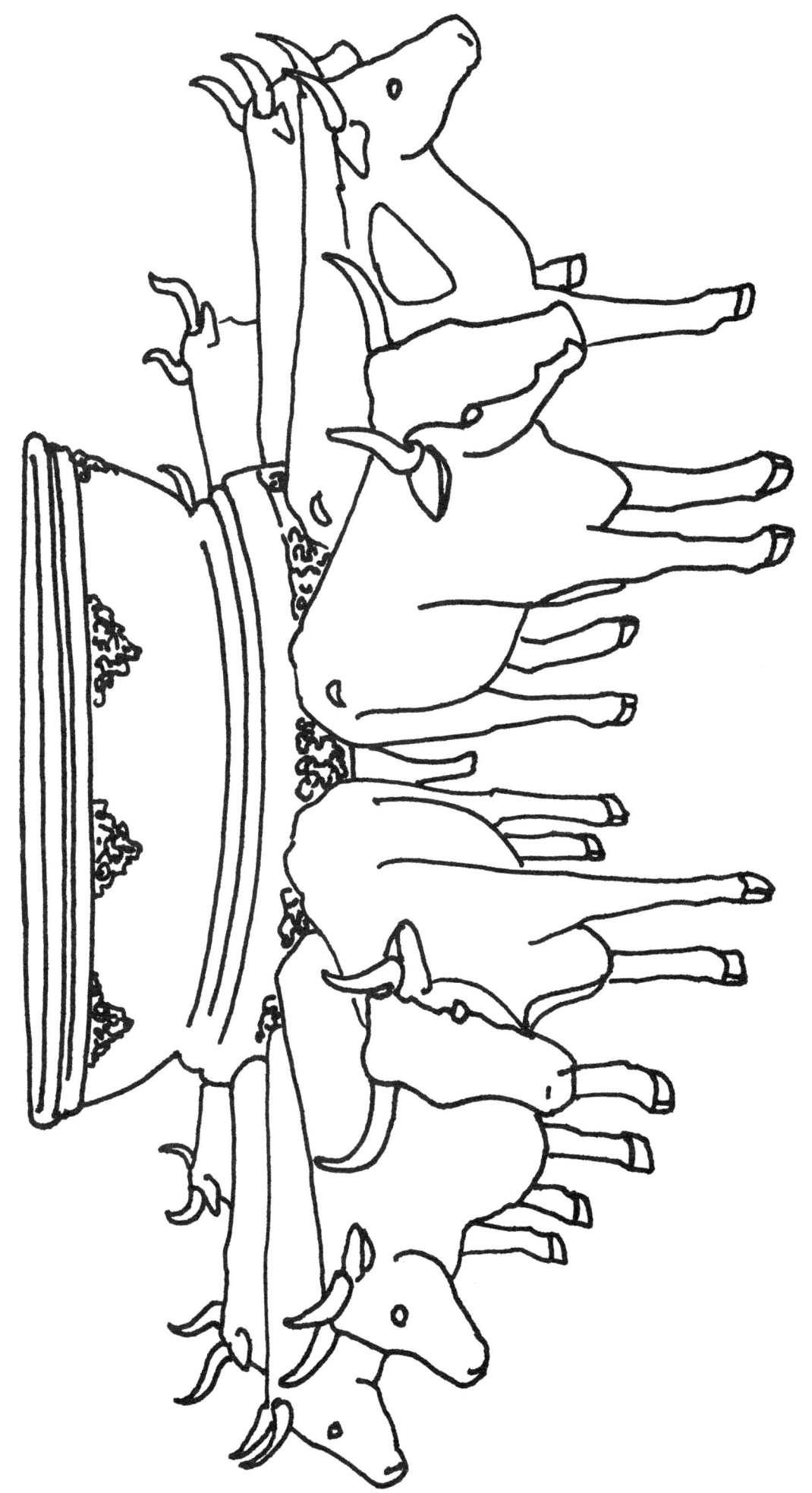

No. 4

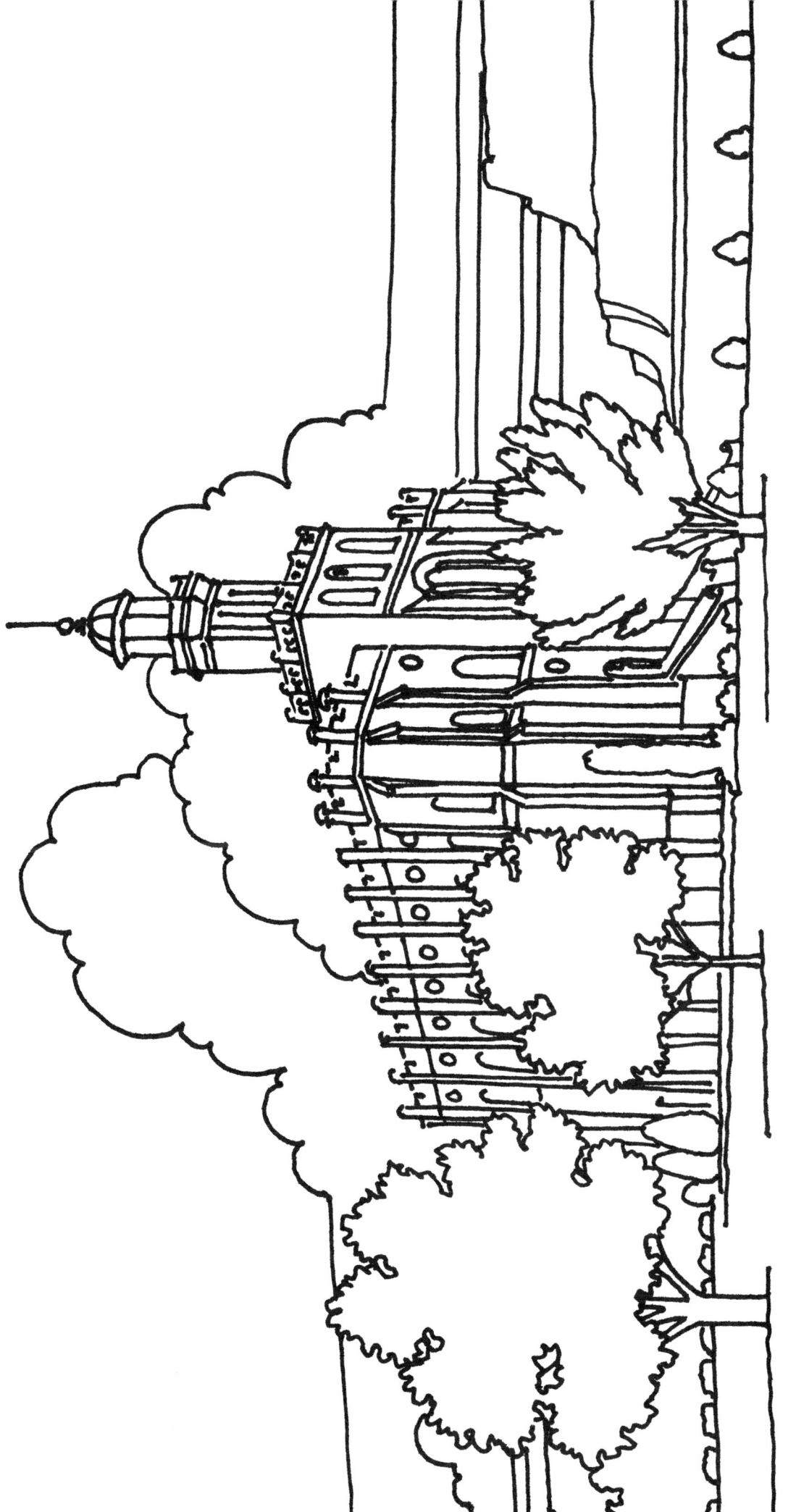

No. 5

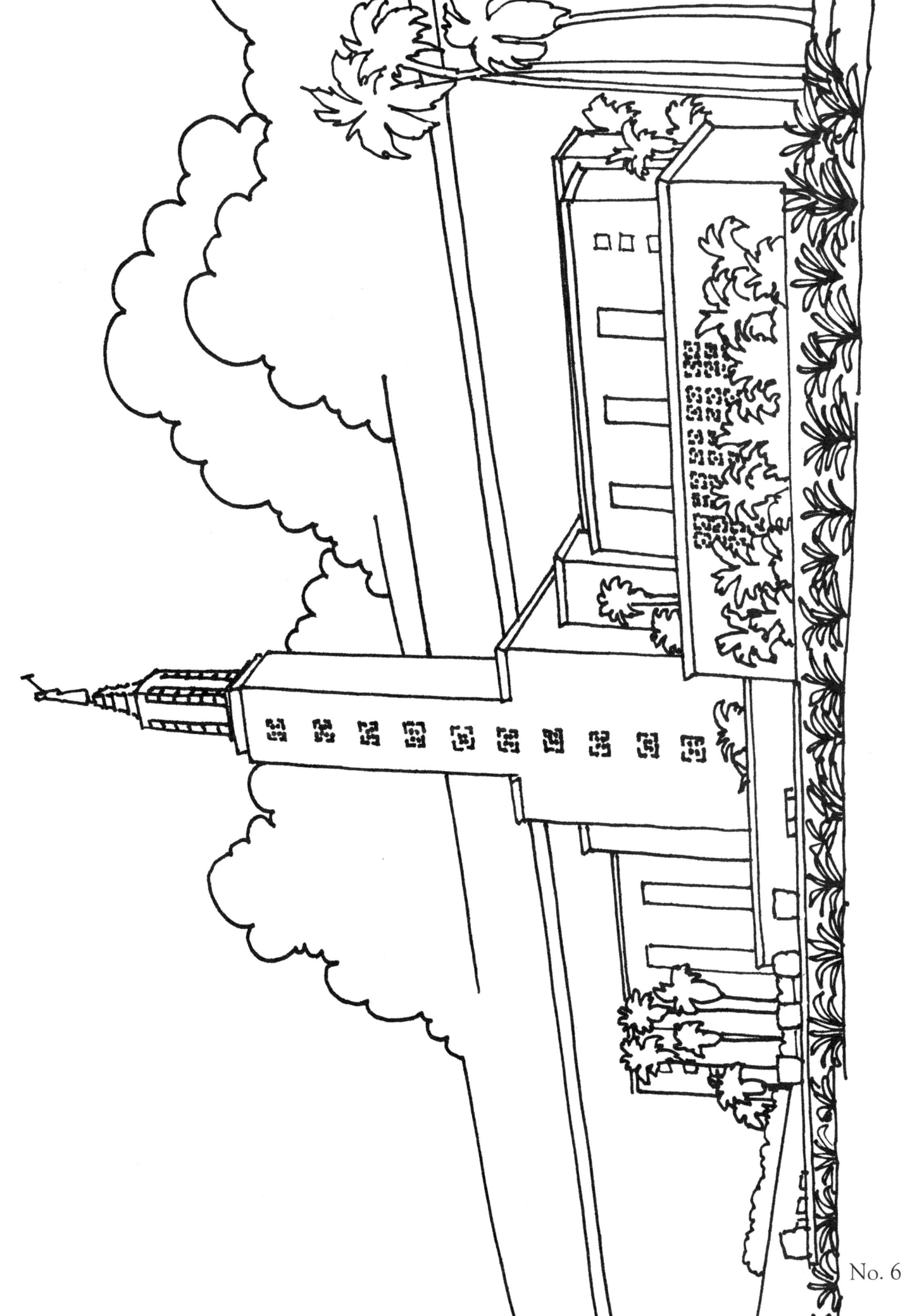

No. 6

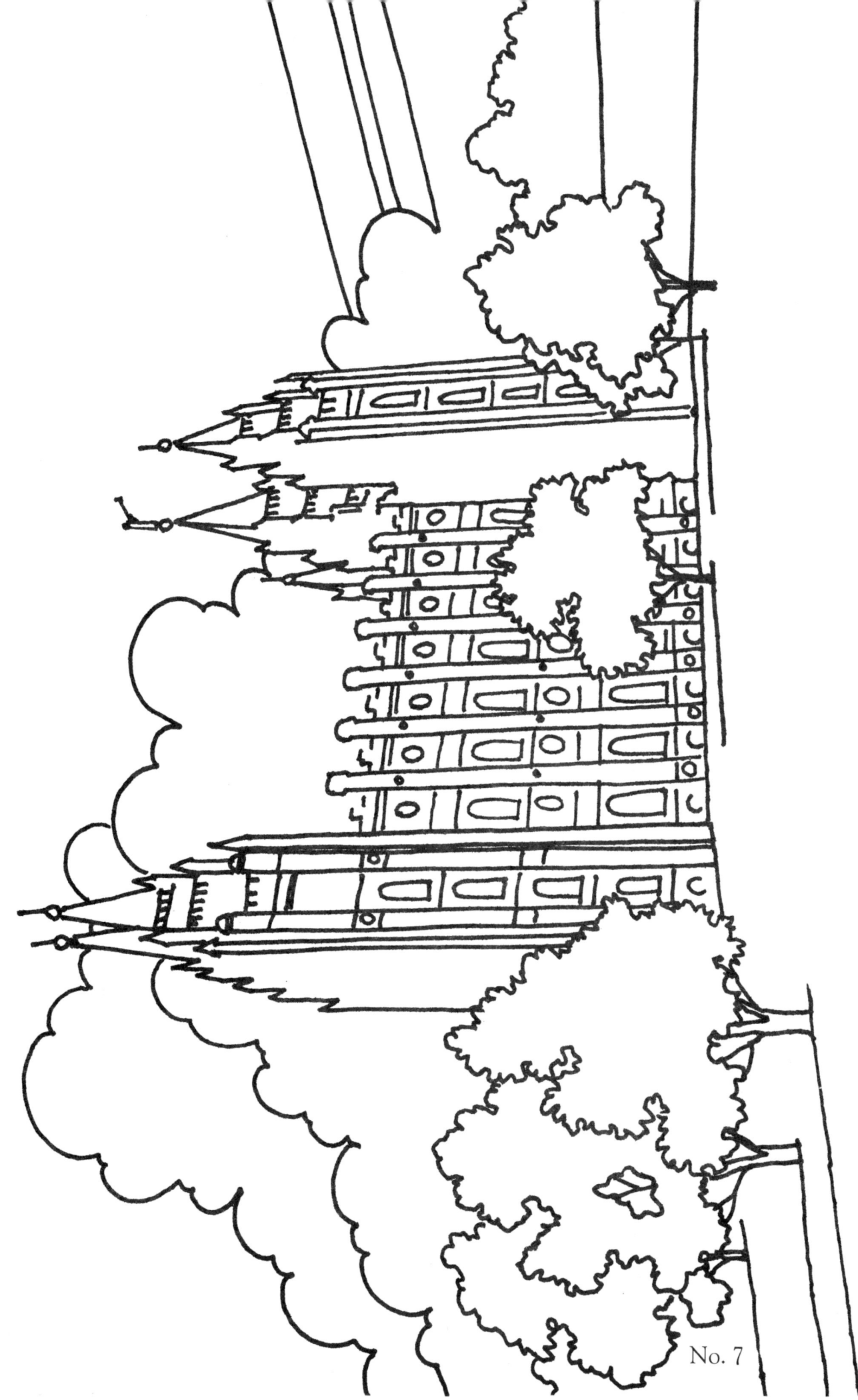

No. 7

No. 8

Presentation 2

Faith—Keeping the Commandments of Heavenly Father

This presentation introduces children to a basic definition of faith—belief in our Heavenly Father. The presenter then explains several ways that faith can be shown to Him. The captions are easily memorized for a more effective presentation.

METHOD ONE (1–6 participants):

Each picture and caption is glued to a separate piece of poster board. This method allows each presentor to take one or more parts.

Materials Needed:
2 poster boards, 24" x 30", any color
photocopies of illustrations and captions to be used (optional)
spray glue, glue stick, or rubber cement
felt-tip markers, colored pencils, or oil pastels
scissors

Directions:
1. Cut each poster board into fourths, making eight separate sheets (two will not be used).
2. Work from photocopies of the original illustrations and captions to keep the book intact for future presentations.
3. Color each picture with felt-tip markers, colored pencils, or oil pastels. (Tip: oil pastels are especially good for skin tones. Use tissue to smooth and blend them.)
4. Glue each picture to a piece of poster board, centering each one and pressing firmly to seal the materials together.
5. Cut each caption along the dotted lines.
6. Glue the appropriate caption in the upper left-hand corner on the back of each mounted picture for easier reading.

METHOD TWO (1–6 participants):

The "cubed" method is fun and adds variety. Seal the flaps of a square box with glue or tape. Cover it with paper or material to make an interesting background. Glue each of the pictures to one of the sides of the box. As the cube is passed from child to child, each one takes a turn saying his or her part and showing the appropriate picture to illustrate it. When this method is used, the captions cannot be glued to the poster boards, so speaking parts must be memorized.

Materials Needed:
1 square box
paper or material to cover the box (optional)
photocopies of illustrations and captions to be used (optional)
spray glue, glue stick, or rubber cement
felt-tip markers, colored pencils, or oil pastels
scissors

Directions:
1. Seal the flaps of the box with glue or tape.
2. Cover the box with paper or material (optional).
3. Work from photocopies of the original illustrations and captions to keep the book intact for future presentations.
4. Color each picture with felt-tip markers, colored pencils, or oil pastels. (Tip: oil pastels are especially good for skin tones. Use tissue to smooth and blend them.)
5. Glue each picture on one face of the cube, centering each one and pressing firmly to seal the materials together.

Leader: Faith is a special kind of belief in our Heavenly Father. We show our faith when we do the things He has asked us to do. Here are some of the ways we can show our faith.

1. Be kind to others.

2. Obey the words of our prophet.

3. Say our prayers.

4. Be honest.

5. Be reverent in church.

6. Read the scriptures.

Leader: Our Heavenly Father loves us when we show our faith in Him by keeping His commandments.

No. 2

No. 3

No. 4

No. 5

No. 6

Presentation 3

Reverence—Showing Love for Heavenly Father

This presentation depicts behavioral situations in church that children will readily relate to. Starting with a picture showing a negative situation, it opens up to show the positive behavior desired. This presentation can be given by the leader or the children.

METHOD ONE (1–4 participants):

This presentation has a negative picture positioned on top of a positive picture, front to back, and both are taped together at the sides. The top picture (negative attitude) is cut down the middle so it can open up to reveal the picture (positive attitude) underneath. The captions for both pictures are glued to the back of the positive picture.

Materials Needed:
2 poster boards, approximately 24" x 30", any color
clear packaging tape
spray glue
felt-tip markers, colored pencils, or oil pastels
scissors
ruler

Directions:
1. Cut poster board into fourths, making eight seperate sheets.
2. Work from photocopies of the original illustrations and captions to keep the book intact for future presentations.
3. Color each picture with felt-tip markers, colored pencils, or oil pastels.(Tip: oil pastels are especially good for skin tones. Use tissue to smooth and blend them.)
4. Glue each picture to a piece of poster board, centering each one and pressing firmly to seal the materials together.
5. Tape pictures 1 and 2 together at the sides. Then tape pictures 3 and 4, 5 and 6, 7 and 8 together as you did pictures 1 and 2.

6. Glue captions for pictures 1 and 2 on the back of picture 2. Glue captions for pictures 3 and 4 on the back of picture 4. Glue captions for pictures 5 and 6 on the back of picture 6.
7. Glue captions for pictures 7 and 8 on the back of picture 8. Mark a straight line down the centers of pictures 1, 3, 5, and 7. Cut along the lines so that the negative pictures on top can open to reveal the positive pictures underneath.

METHOD TWO (1–8 participants):

Each picture and caption is glued to a separate piece of poster board. This method may be used with each person taking one or more parts.

Materials Needed:
2 poster boards, approximately 24" x 30", any color
photocopies of illustrations and captions to be used (optional)
spray glue, glue stick, or rubber cement
felt-tip markers, colored pencils, or oil pastels
scissors

Directions:
1. Cut each poster board into fourths, making eight separate sheets.
2. Work from photocopies of the original illustrations and captions to keep the book intact for future presentations.
3. Color each picture with felt-tip markers, colored pencils, or oil pastels. (Tip: oil pastels are especially good for skin tones. Use tissue to smooth and blend them.)
4. Glue each picture to a piece of poster board, centering each one and pressing firmly to seal the materials together.
5. Cut each caption along the dotted lines.
6. Glue the appropriate caption in the left-hand corner on the back of each mounted picture for easy reading.

Leader: We are all children of our Heavenly Father. When we come to Primary, we show our love for Him when we act our very best. Here are some children who come to Primary. Let's see if you know who really loves Heavenly Father best.

1. When these children come to Primary, they push and shove to get to their chairs.

2. But other children show respect by walking quietly and reverently.

3. These children throw paper onto the floor, making our church very messy!

4. But other children carefully place their scraps of paper in the nearest wastebasket.

5. These children write in the songbooks and place their feet on the benches.

6. But other children sing their very best and keep their feet on the floor.

7. These children talk and sometimes even shout when Primary leaders are talking.

8. But other children listen carefully and raise their hands to answer when their Primary leaders call upon them.

Leader: Yes, it is easy to see which children love their Heavenly Father by the way they show reverence in Primary.

No. 1

No. 2

No. 3

No. 4

No. 5

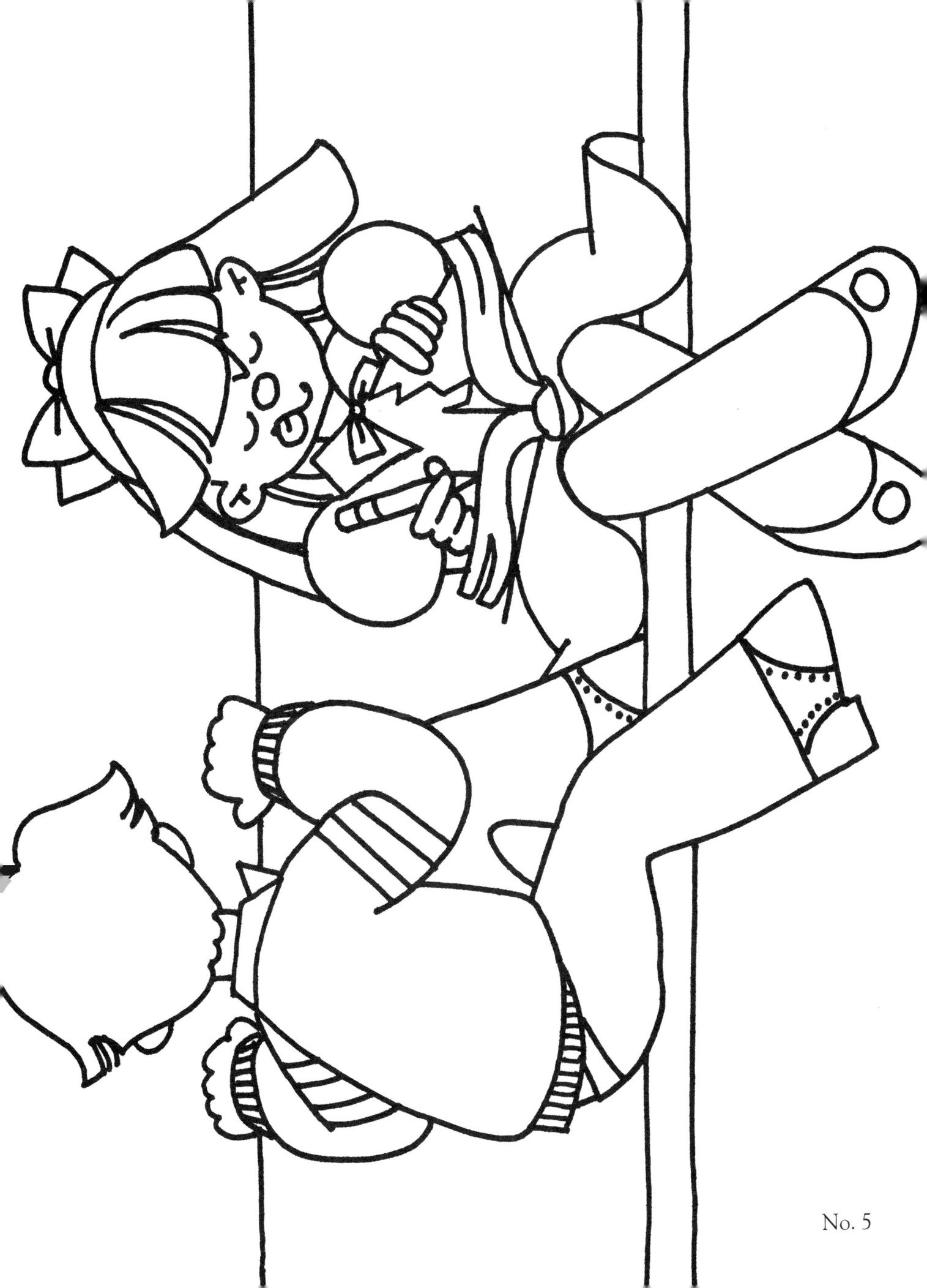

No. 6

No. 7

No. 8

Presentation 4
Prayer—Drawing Closer to Heavenly Father

This presentation teaches children the various times when prayers may be offered. They also learn about different kinds of prayer—personal, sacrament, baptism, blessing the food, etc. It reinforces the principle of praying often and why it is so important for us to converse with Heavenly Father continually.

METHOD ONE (1–6 participants):

Each piece of poster board has a picture pasted on both the front and back. A wooden stick is taped to the bottom of each poster board for a handle. This makes it easy to turn the picture around to see the next picture in sequence. When this method is used, the captions cannot be glued to the poster boards, so parts must be memorized.

Materials Needed:
2 poster boards, approximately 24" x 30", any color
photocopies of illustrations and captions to be used (optional)
spray glue, glue stick, or rubber cement
6 wooden popsicle sticks or tongue depressors
felt-tip markers, colored pencils, or oil pastels
scissors

Directions:
1. Cut each poster board into fourths, making eight separate sheets (two will not be used).
2. Work from photocopies of the original illustrations and captions to keep the book intact for future presentations.
3. Color each picture with felt-tip markers, colored pencils, or oil pastels. (Tip: oil pastels are especially good for skin tones. Use tissue to smooth and blend them.)
4. Spread glue on the backs of pictures 1 and 2. Center each one on a piece of poster board, back-to-back, and press firmly to seal all materials together. Then continue this same method for the remaining pictures.
5. Tape a wooden stick to the bottom of each poster board for a handle. This makes it easy to turn the picture around.

METHOD TWO (1–12 participants):

Each picture and caption is pasted on a separate piece of poster board. As many as twelve children can participate, or one child or a leader can hold up each picture as the dialogue is presented.

Materials Needed:
3 poster boards, approximately 24" x 30", any color
photocopies of illustrations and captions to be used (optional)
spray glue, glue stick, or rubber cement
felt-tip markers, colored pencils, or oil pastels
scissors

Directions:
1. Cut each poster board into fourths, making twelve separate sheets.
2. Work from photocopies of the original illustrations and captions to keep the book intact for future presentations.
3. Color each picture with felt-tip markers, colored pencils, or oil pastels. (Tip: oil pastels are especially good for skin tones. Use tissue to smooth and blend them.)
4. Glue each picture to a piece of poster board, centering each one and pressing firmly to seal the materials together.
5. Cut each caption along the dotted lines.
6. Glue the appropriate caption in the upper left-hand corner on the back of each mounted picture for easy reading.

Leader: Heavenly Father is a real person who loves us. He has great wisdom, knowledge, and power. We can talk to Him through prayer whenever we need Him.

1. in the morning

2. at night

3. when we are in church

4. before we take the sacrament

5. when we are baptized

6. when we are confirmed

7. when we are given a name and a blessing

8. when we are sick

9. in hard times

10. in happy times

11. before we eat our food

12. when our families are together

Leader: Prayer is a wonderful way of getting close to Heavenly Father and receiving His many blessings.

No. 1

No. 2

No. 3

No. 4

No. 5

No. 6

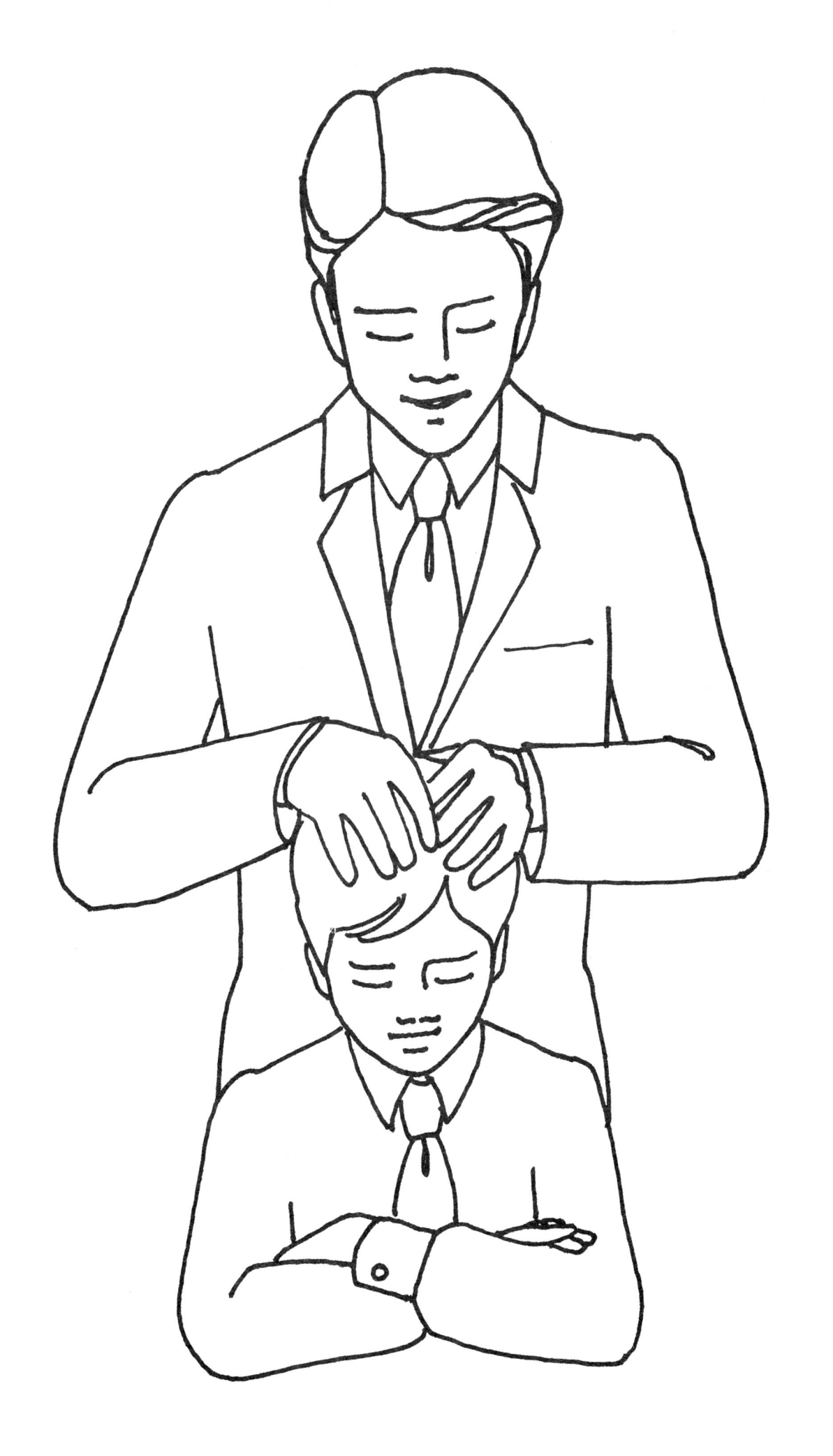

No. 7

No. 8

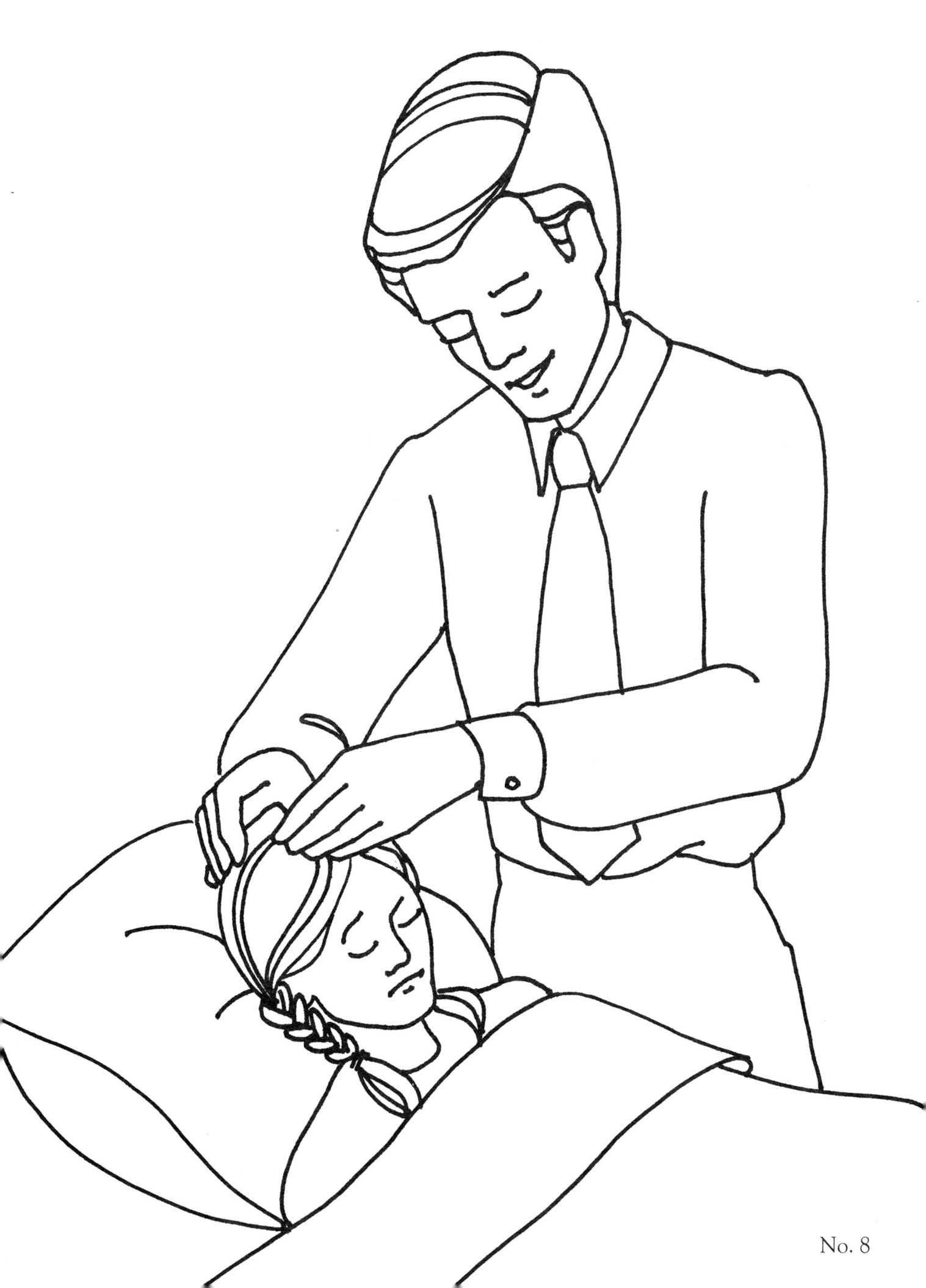

No. 9

No. 10

No. 11

No. 12